HOW TO BE A KID AGAIN

Jim Baker

books by Jim Baker

HOW OUR COUNTIES GOT THEIR NAMES

THE BIG DITCH

THE WAYS OF THE WARRIORS

CABIN IN THE CLEARING

FRONTIER MEDICINE

NAMING THE STATES

TRAINS OF YESTERYEAR

GET OUT AND GET UNDER

HOW TO BE A KID AGAIN

First Edition, April, 1974
Second Edition, October, 1975

Copyright © 1974, 1975 by Jim Baker
Worthington, Ohio

All rights reserved. No part of this publication may be reproduced without written permission from the publisher, except by a reviewer who may quote brief passages or reproduce illustrations in a review; nor may any part of this book be reproduced, stored in a retrieval system, or transmitted in any form or by any means electronic, photocopying, recording or other, without written permission from the publisher.
Produced in the United States of America.

A Heartland House book, published by
PERIODS & COMMAS, Marlton, NJ 08053

Library of Congress Catalog Card Number: 74-76723
International Standard Book Number: 0-914482-07-6

For
Barb and Jim and John and Beth.
I wish that we were all kids again.

HOW TO BE A KID AGAIN

FOREWORD!

ONE AFTERNOON ON THE WAY HOME FROM SCHOOL, DICK FREELAND ANNOUNCED THAT RUTHIE PASSWATER WAS "HIS GIRL." THEN, ANTICIPATING THE HOOTS AND JEERS THAT WERE CERTAIN TO FOLLOW, HE ADDED HASTILY, "YOU OUGHTA SEE HER WHEN SHE'S DRESSED UP!" LIKE RUTHIE, THOSE DEPRESSION YEARS WHEN WE WERE GROWING UP DON'T LOOK HALF BAD WHEN "DRESSED UP". IN RETROSPECT, WE TEND TO SEE ONLY THE SPARKLE IN THE EYE, IGNORING THE WART ON THE NOSE.

THE MERE FACT THAT WE WERE KIDS INSULATED US FROM MANY OF THE GRIMMER ASPECTS OF THOSE BITTER TIMES. WHILE OUR PARENTS STRUGGLED TO STAY OUT OF THE BREAD LINES, WE WENT ON OUR MERRY WAY, TAKING OUR FUN WHERE WE FOUND IT. IF WE WERE DEPRIVED, MOST OF US DIDN'T KNOW ABOUT IT— ON THE CONTRARY, FROM A KID'S POINT OF VIEW, IT IS PERFECTLY REASONABLE TO SAY, "THOSE WERE THE DAYS".

FOR ONE THING, WE ENJOYED THE DISTINCT ADVANTAGE OF BEING LEFT ALONE. NOT IGNORED; LEFT ALONE—THERE'S A GREAT DIFFERENCE! IT HAD NOT YET BECOME FASHIONABLE FOR YOUNG FOLKS' LIVES TO BE PROGRAMMED BY "EXPERTS." STILL IN THE FUTURE WAS THE ABSURDITY OF A GROUP OF ADULTS SITTING AROUND A TABLE DECIDING THAT SUCH AND SUCH A GAME WAS "SUITABLE FOR AGES THREE TO SIX;" THAT TOY **X** (SCIENTIFICALLY ENGINEERED, EASILY ASSEMBLED, BATTERIES NOT INCLUDED) WAS JUST THE TICKET FOR TWELVE-YEAR-OLDS. WE WERE ALLOWED TO DETERMINE OUR OWN DIVERSIONS AND TO CONSTRUCT OUR OWN PLAYTHINGS WITH COMPLETE AUTONOMY SO LONG AS WE DIDN'T PUT SOMEBODY'S EYE OUT OR TRAMPLE THE FLOWER BEDS.

Some of the things we made were extremely simple; others fairly complex. Some are still known and popular today while others have vanished without a trace.

Left to his own devices and permitted to give free rein to his imagination, a child will often come up with rather remarkable accomplishments... As an additional impetus, a sort of empty-pockets ingenuity was forced upon us by those lean years and we responded with amazing inventiveness. This is not to say that contemporary kids would not do just as well, but our present affluence hasn't demanded as

much from them and even if it did, they would be seriously handicapped by today's unimaginative trash heaps. A casual stroll down any neighborhood alley in the thirties never failed to yield an old tire, a couple of innertubes, a broken umbrella—all treasured items and the raw materials for our manufactories.

Some of the finished products will be examined in the following pages. While most of them were home-made, some few had to be purchased, either completely or in part, with carefully hoarded capital (we weren't entirely without money). Some of the

things we played with have been omitted because of their obviously lethal aspects (we built a pistol with gas pipe and firecrackers that would curl your hair!) Others, such as "BB" guns and fireworks, get scant attention since they have been largely legislated away. Mostly, we've attempted to recall those playthings that were enjoyable, relatively harmless, and common in our neighborhood forty years ago. Some you may recognize; others might be unfamiliar. Glaring omissions may occur to you. But, in any case, it is our hope that you will find it pleasant to play with them—albeit vicariously—once again.

We'll meet in the vacant lot right after school, so—"ask your mother can you come out and play!"

Jim Baker

TIN CAN "TOM WALKERS"

DID ANYTHING EVER PRODUCE A MORE SOUL-SATISFYING RACKET THAN "TOM WALKERS" ON CONCRETE?

TOM WALKERS WERE MADE BY STOMPING ON A TIN CAN. ONE GOOD TROMP COLLAPSED THE CAN FIRMLY AROUND THE HEEL OF YOUR SHOE... IN ADDITION TO MAKING ENOUGH NOISE TO WAKE THE DEAD, TOM WALKERS COULD BE MADE TO STRIKE SPARKS WHEN YOU KIND OF SCOOTED THEM ALONG THE SIDEWALK.

-**A**ND WHEN YOU GOT TIRED OF THEM, A GOOD KICK AGAINST THE CURB KNOCKED 'EM OFF.

INNERTUBE ARTILLERY

Many of our "cops and robbers" and "cowboys and indians" battles were fought with our trusty innertube pistols. Within its short range this arm was also a decent target gun — you could knock over a tin can, if it was close enough.

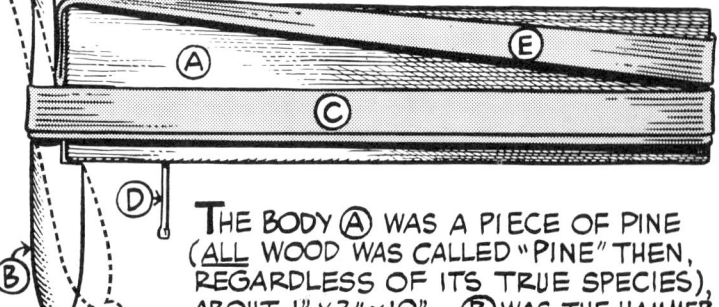

The body Ⓐ was a piece of pine (ALL wood was called "pine" then, regardless of its true species), about 1" x 3" x 10"... Ⓑ was the hammer, made from half a clothespin, held in place by innertube tension bands Ⓒ.

The gun was fired by squeezing the finish-nail trigger Ⓓ. This forced the hammer forward releasing the "bullet" band Ⓔ. The tighter the tension of the bands Ⓒ and Ⓔ the greater the velocity.

CUT BANDS ABOUT 5/8" WIDE

BIG BUBBLES

WE USED TO BLOW SOAP BUBBLES AS BIG AS BEACH BALLS, USING AN OLD INNERTUBE AS THE "BLOWER-UPPER"...(THIS WAS STRICTLY AN OUTDOOR ACTIVITY; MOTHERS DIDN'T LIKE THESE THINGS IN THE HOUSE!)

WE MADE A SLIT IN THE INNERTUBE AND INSERTED A SECOND VALVE (WITH CORE REMOVED) BESIDE THE ONE ALREADY THERE. THIS WAS SEALED WITH TIRE PATCHING CEMENT. TO THIS VALVE WE ATTACHED ABOUT 3 FEET OF SMALL RUBBER TUBING. AT THE OTHER END OF THE TUBING A SMALL CLAY BUBBLE PIPE WAS INSERTED. A SPRING TYPE CLOTHES PIN WAS USED ON THE TUBING AS AN AIR CUT-OFF VALVE. THE PIPE WAS DIPPED IN SOAPY WATER (WITH GLYCERINE ADDED), THE CLOTHES PIN RELEASED — AND LET 'ER RIP!

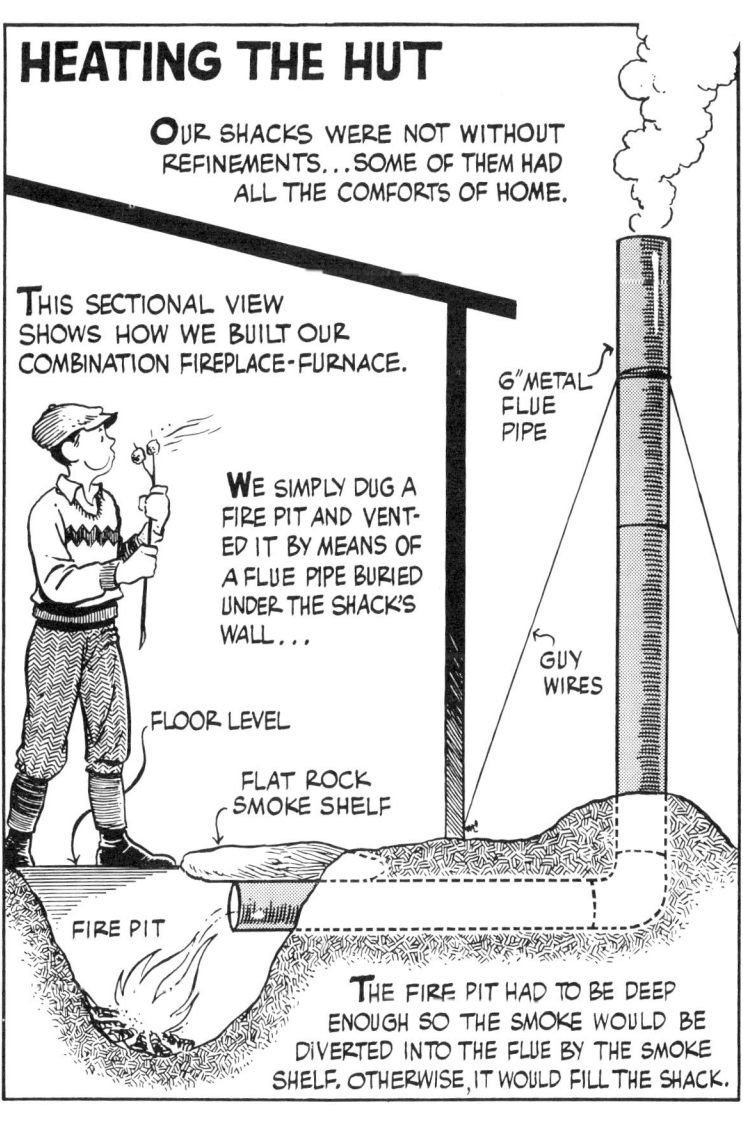

TANK CORPS

IF YOU NEVER TOOK PART IN SPOOL-TANK RACES ACROSS THE LIVING ROOM RUG YOURS WAS A DEPRIVED CHILDHOOD... VERY SIMPLE TO MAKE, TANKS REQUIRED ONLY A SPOOL, A SMALL CHUNK OF SOAP, A RUBBER BAND, AND A FEW WOODEN MATCHSTICKS.

BUILD THE TANK THUS:

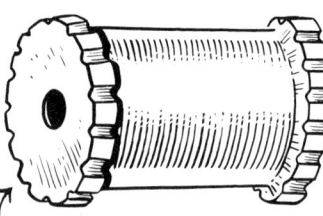

① BEGIN BY NOTCHING "TREADS" AROUND ENDS OF SPOOL. (THE TANK WILL WORK WITHOUT THE NOTCHES, BUT WON'T CLIMB).

② CUT "GEAR" FROM SOAP (ABOUT 3/16" THICK). CUT CENTER HOLE AND RUB GROOVE AS SHOWN

③ RUBBER BAND SHOULD BE SLIGHTLY SHORTER THAN SPOOL. (PICK A WIDE ONE).

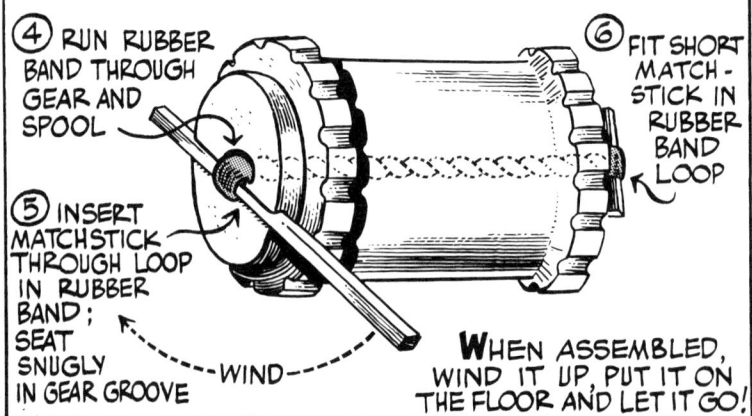

④ RUN RUBBER BAND THROUGH GEAR AND SPOOL

⑤ INSERT MATCHSTICK THROUGH LOOP IN RUBBER BAND; SEAT SNUGLY IN GEAR GROOVE

⑥ FIT SHORT MATCHSTICK IN RUBBER BAND LOOP

--WIND--

WHEN ASSEMBLED, WIND IT UP, PUT IT ON THE FLOOR AND LET IT GO!

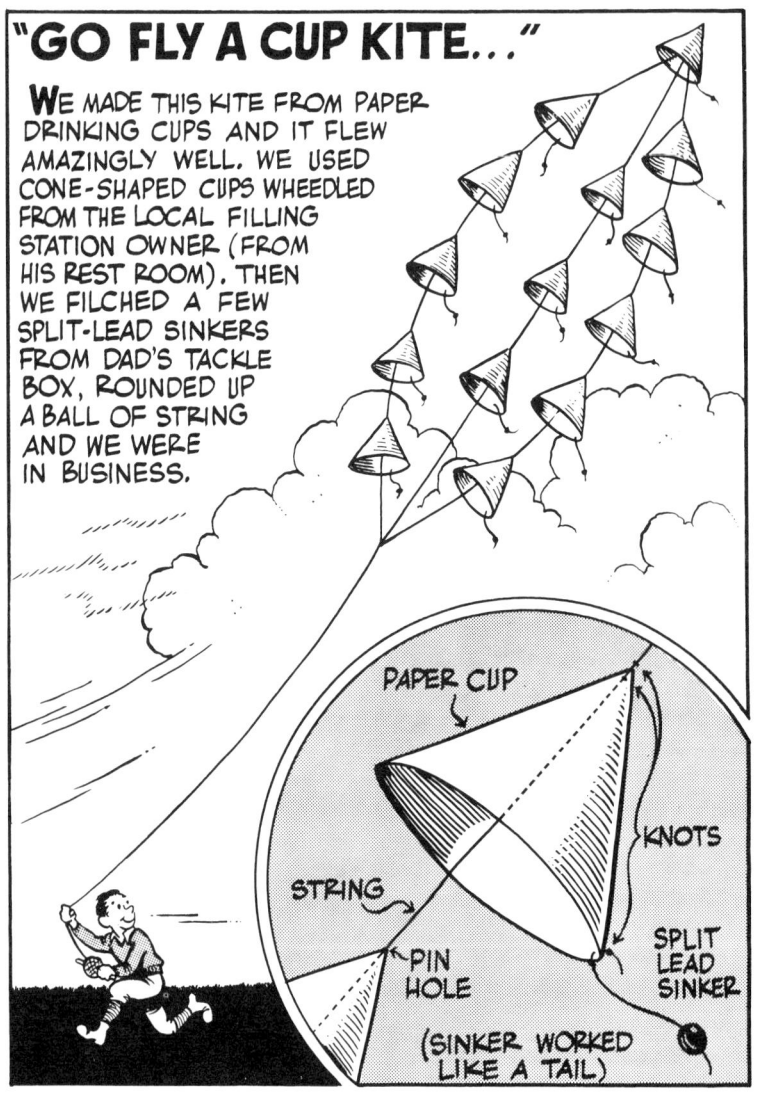

POTATO PRINTING

One of our inside-on-a-rainy-day activities was potato printing... (This was a short-term project, usually holding our attention an hour or two.)

Begin by choosing a fairly large and longish potato... cut it in half (this gives you two uniform "type" surfaces.)

Cut relief letters about 1/4" high. Make sure they're reversed or they will print backwards.

Ink your tater on a stamp pad and print!

Our potato printing was a small operation, seldom more than a couple of letters. There was no way to con mom out of enough spuds for a whole alphabet!

JACK KNIFE BASEBALL

All you needed was a jack knife... you could even be both "teams" if no other player was available.

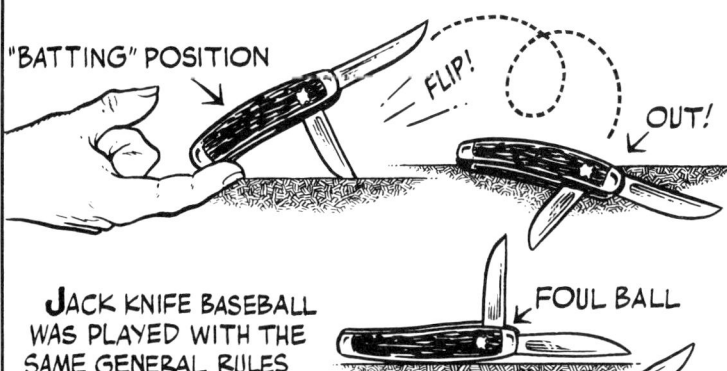

"BATTING" POSITION — FLIP! — OUT!

Jack knife baseball was played with the same general rules that governed the real game — nine innings, three outs, and so on...

Extra base hits were a lot easier to make if the ground wasn't too dry...

The secret of "batting" was to make sure that the short blade wasn't jammed into the ground too firmly.

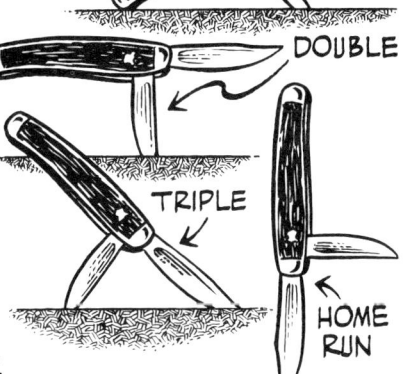

FOUL BALL — SINGLE — DOUBLE — TRIPLE — HOME RUN

THE ENDLESS VARIATIONS OF
MUMBLY PEG

MUMBLY PEG, LIKE "BASEBALL", WAS A GAME PLAYED WITH A POCKET KNIFE. FOR MUMBLY PEG WE USED THE THIN, DULL-POINTED BLADE (WE CALLED IT A "LEATHER PUNCH") OF ONE OF THOSE MULTI-BLADE "SCOUT" KNIVES.

THE OBJECT OF MUMBLY PEG WAS SIMPLE: YOU FLIPPED THE KNIFE SO THAT IT STUCK IN THE GROUND. STARTING WITH EASY POSITIONS, YOU PROGRESSED THROUGH INCREASINGLY TOUGHER FLIPS. AS LONG AS THE KNIFE STUCK, YOU CONTINUED. WHEN YOU MISSED, IT BECAME THE NEXT PLAYER'S TURN — UNLESS YOU DECIDED TO "CHANCE IT". THIS GAVE YOU A SECOND CHANCE; IF YOU MADE IT,

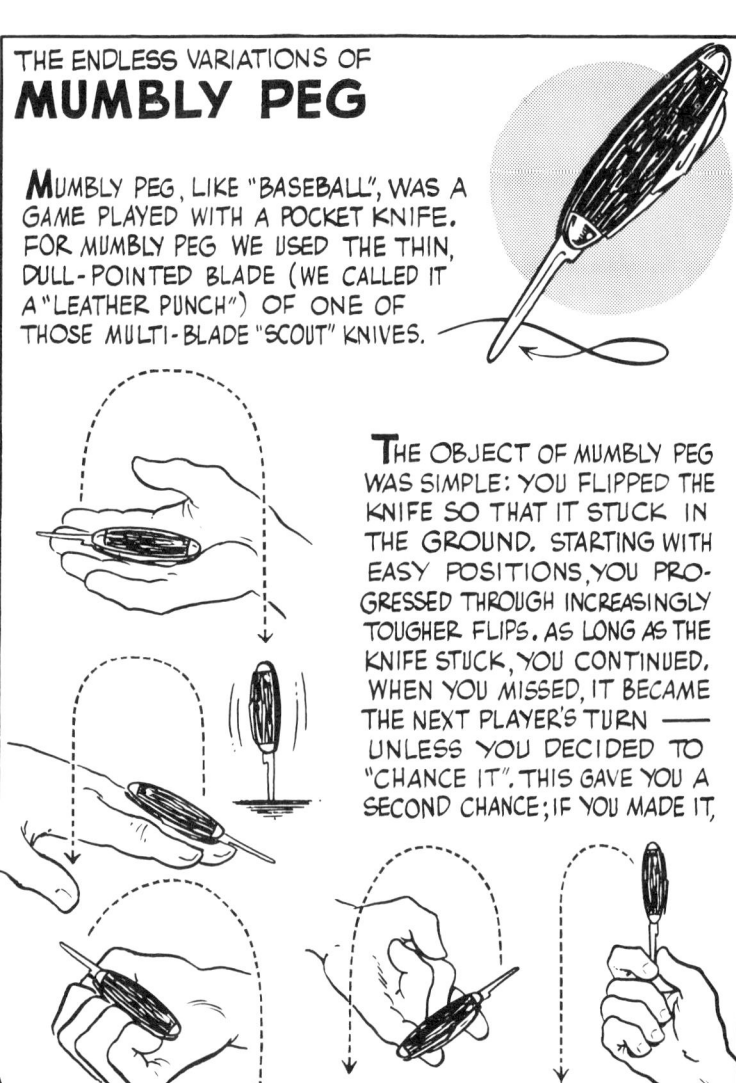

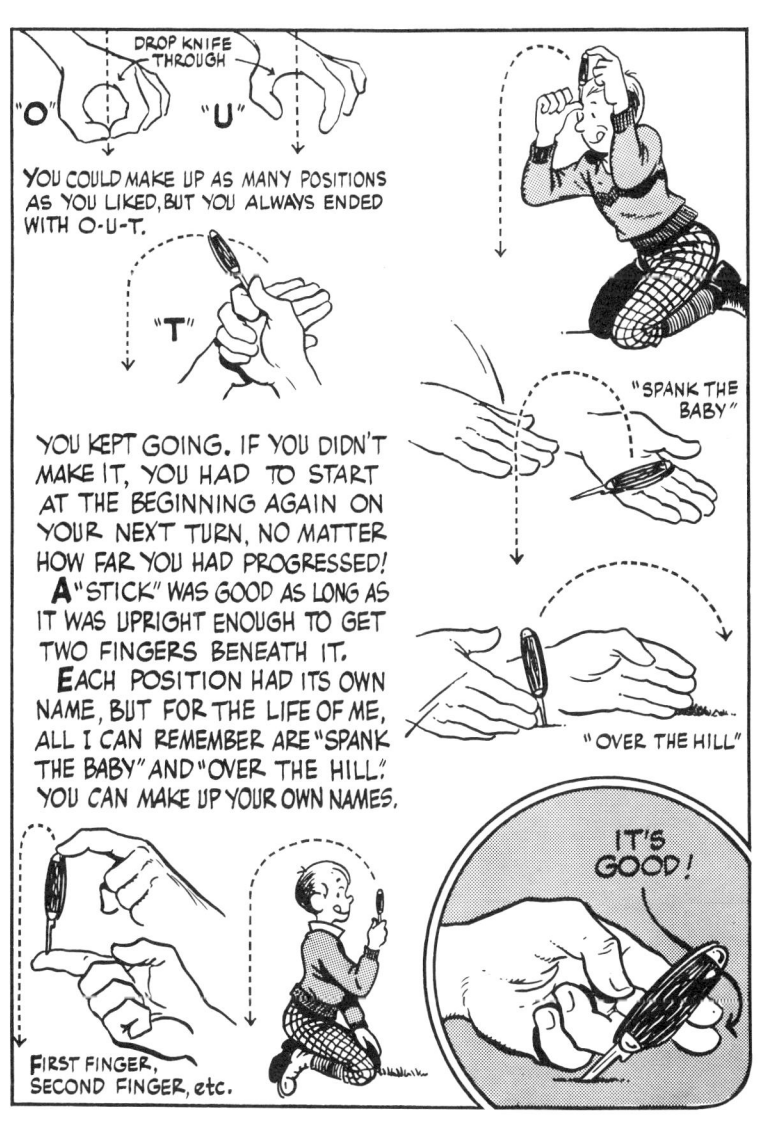

BUCKEYE BEADS
SINCE WE GOT OUR "RAISIN'" IN THE MIDWEST WHERE BUCKEYES WERE COMMON, WE PUT THEM TO MANY USES. THE GIRLS FAVORED THEM FOR JEWELRY. BUCKEYES MADE A BEAUTIFUL "STRING OF BEADS" THAT COULD BE ASSEMBLED IN MINUTES.

← ORDINARY HOUSEHOLD TWINE

BUCKEYES WERE PIERCED WITH AN ICE PICK (OR A NAIL).

A COMBINATION OF BUCKEYES AND ELBOW MACARONI MADE AN ESPECIALLY FINE NECKLACE.

← STICK 'EM SO THE "EYE" WILL BE FACING OUT WHEN STRUNG.

REGARDING BUCKEYES: WE WERE CAREFUL TO KEEP THEM AWAY FROM OUR MOUTHS. I HAVE NO IDEA WHETHER OR NOT IT'S TRUE, BUT WE ALWAYS THOUGHT THEY WERE POISON!

THE REAL THING

NO MATTER HOW CONVINCINGLY YOU MIGHT DECLARE YOUR UNDYING AFFECTION FOR THAT PRETTY GIRL WITH THE BLUE EYES AND LONG CURLS, SHE DIDN'T BELIEVE YOU UNTIL SHE HAD TANGIBLE EVIDENCE. SO YOU SLIPPED A **CIGAR BAND** ON HER FINGER AND YOU WERE CONSIDERED ENGAGED, FOREVER AND EVER — MAYBE EVEN A WEEK!

OH, WILBUR— A "HABANA IMPERIALE"!

NOTHIN' BUT THE BEST FOR YOU, AMY!

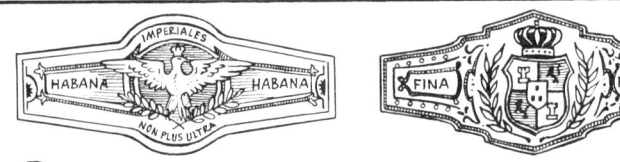

BEAUTIFULLY EMBOSSED, AND RICH WITH GOLD AND BRIGHT COLOR, CIGAR BANDS WERE VERY SHOWY ARTICLES.

WE CALLED IT "CATTY"

—ALTHOUGH IT MAY HAVE BEEN "CADDY."
I HAVE NO IDEA HOW IT WAS SPELLED;
ONLY THE WAY WE PRONOUNCED IT.
EITHER WAY IT WAS GREAT FUN.
WE BEGAN BY WHITTLING
POINTED ENDS ON A PIECE
OF 2"x2" ABOUT 9" LONG.
THE CENTER SECTION
WAS LEFT SQUARE AND
NUMBERED 1,2,3,4...

WE PLAYED "CATTY" ACROSS A PLAYGROUND WITH A STARTING LINE AT ONE SIDE AND A GOAL LINE AT THE OTHER (PERHAPS 200 YARDS DISTANT).

YOU STUCK THE STICK IN THE GROUND, KIND OF "GOLFED" IT UP IN THE AIR WITH A PADDLE, AND HIT IT FOR DISTANCE BEFORE IT HIT THE GROUND.

THE NUMBER SHOWING ON THE TOP FACE OF THE STICK WHERE IT LANDED INDICATED THE NUMBER OF WHACKS YOU GOT ON YOUR NEXT TURN ("3" UP, YOU GOT 3 HITS).

THE FIRST PLAYER TO HIT HIS STICK ACROSS THE GOAL WAS THE WINNER.

FIRST CAR

After we outgrew our orange crate scooters ("kid stuff") we graduated to orange crate cars. Normally, the first "car" was a very basic vehicle, with subsequent ones becoming increasingly complex.

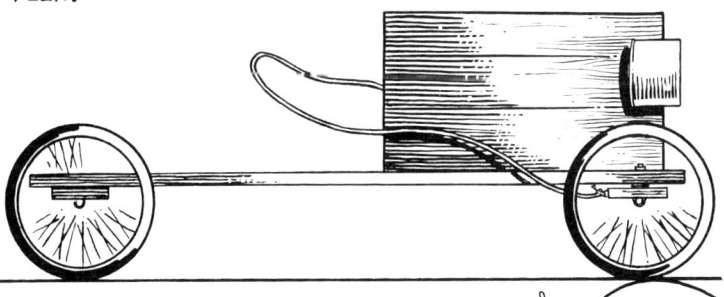

Your basic orange crate racer consisted of a crate (hood) mounted on a floor board, front and rear axle support boards, 4 wheels and a clothesline "steering wheel". The rear axle board was rigid, while the front was attached with bolt and washers for turning.

The greatest problem was conning someone into pushing you.

"I WANT A TURN!"

"PUSH!!"

NEW AND IMPROVED

As we grew a little older the simple orange crate car was no longer adequate. The next step was usually a fancier body, followed by such refinements as a more dependable steering system, brakes, etc...

A fine steering arrangement could be made from an old coaster-wagon wheel, some sash cord or clothesline and a few screweyes...

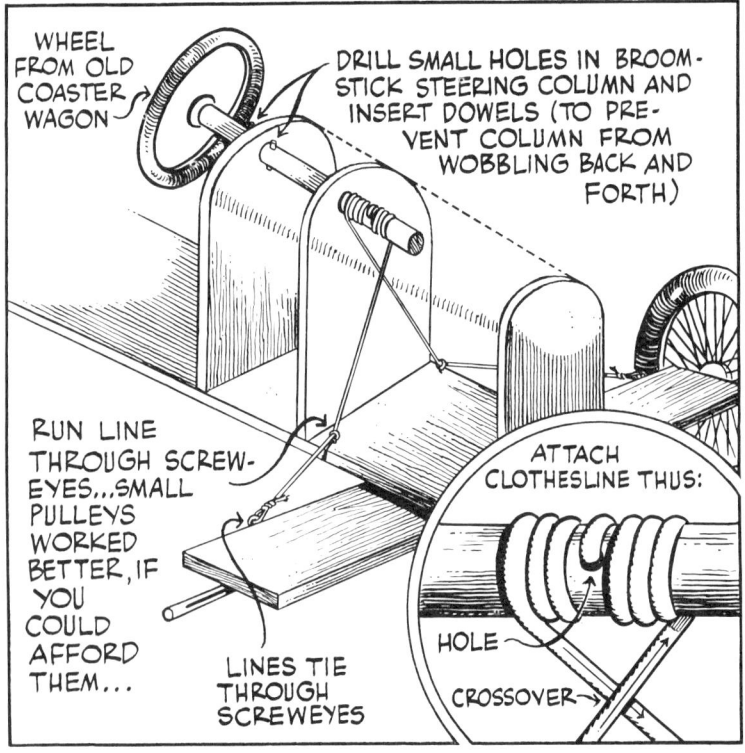

PERFECTION!

With its redesigned body and improved steering our racer had nearly reached the peak of perfection. The final touch was a brake system. There were many styles, but this four-wheel arrangement worked best.

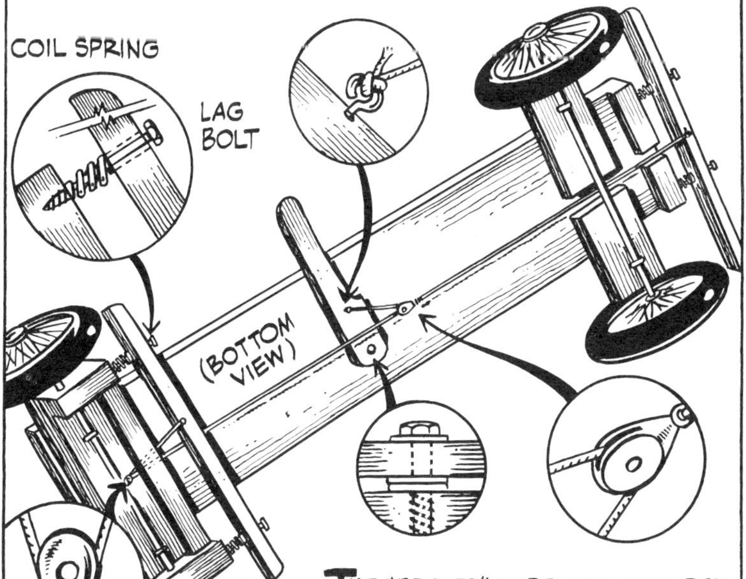

COIL SPRING

LAG BOLT

(BOTTOM VIEW)

The "brakes" were two wooden bars held away from the wheels by coil springs and actuated by sash cord and pulleys connected to a foot pedal.

When the foot was applied to the pedal, the springs compressed bringing the brakes into contact with the wheels providing a quick, even stop.

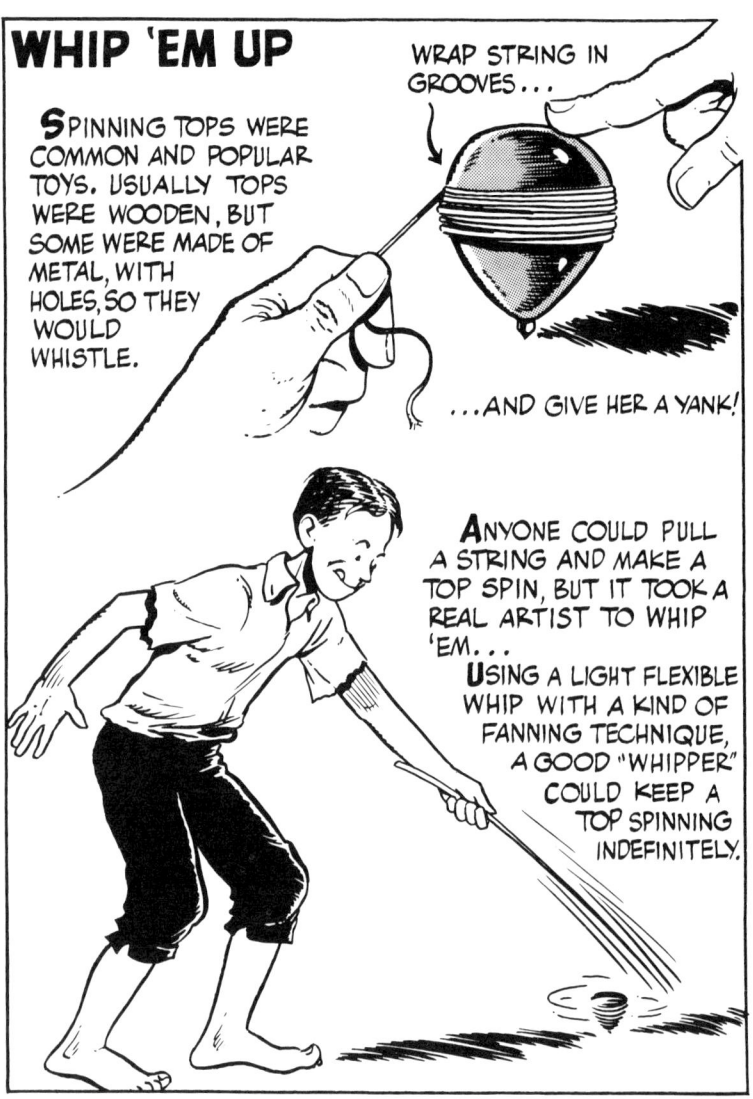

BUCKEYE "CLICKERS"

IF YOU ARE EASILY FRUSTRATED OR HAVE A SHORT TEMPER, DON'T MESS AROUND WITH "CLICKERS"; THEY WILL DRIVE YOU UP THE WALL! TWO BUCKEYES WERE DRILLED AND TIED TO EACH END OF A STRING A COUPLE OF FEET LONG. HOLDING THE STRING IN THE CENTER, YOU TRIED TO SWING ONE BUCKEYE CLOCKWISE, THE OTHER COUNTER-CLOCKWISE... IT WAS A TOUGH EXERCISE IN COORDINATION!

CLICK!

CLICK!

THE OBJECT WAS TO MAKE THE BUCKEYES CLICK TOGETHER AT THE TOP AND BOTTOM OF EACH ARC. WHEN PROPERLY DONE, YOU GOT A RAPID AND STEADY "CLICK, CLICK, CLICK".

BUCKEYES WERE IDEAL AS WEIGHTS: HEAVY ENOUGH TO WORK, YET LIGHT ENOUGH THAT THEY DIDN'T KNOCK YOU FLAT IF THEY HIT YOU!

TAKE ONE BUSTED BUMBERSHOOT

An examination of neighborhood trash barrels nearly always produced at least one broken umbrella. A "busted bumbershoot" provided material for all kinds of ingenious devices, such as this bow and arrow...

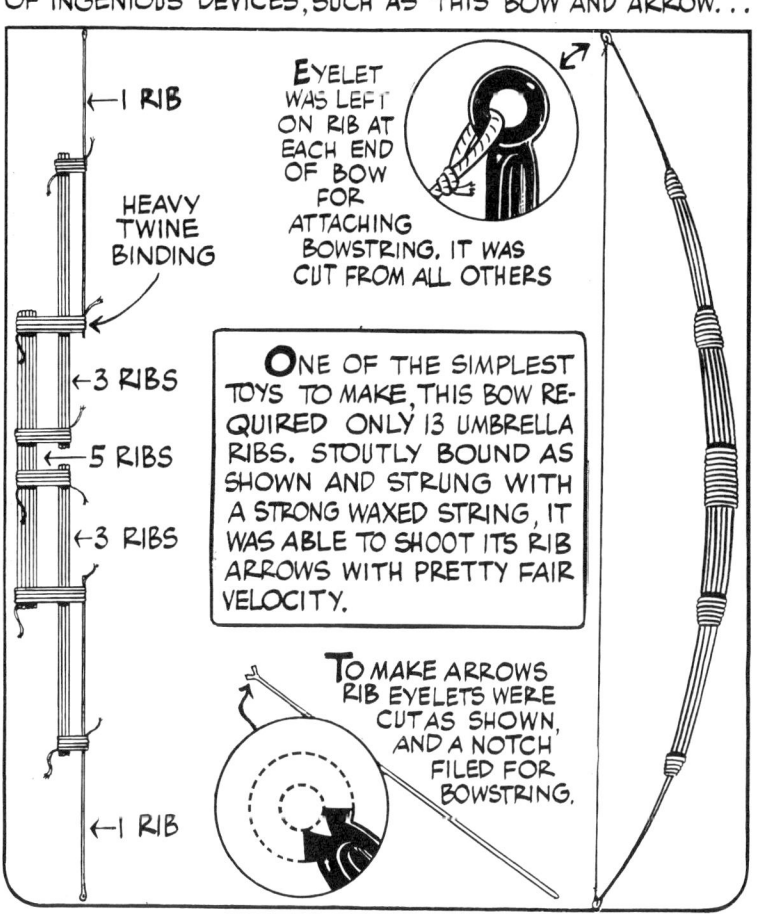

← 1 RIB

HEAVY TWINE BINDING

Eyelet was left on rib at each end of bow for attaching bowstring. It was cut from all others

← 3 RIBS

← 5 RIBS

← 3 RIBS

One of the simplest toys to make, this bow required only 13 umbrella ribs. Stoutly bound as shown and strung with a strong waxed string, it was able to shoot its rib arrows with pretty fair velocity.

← 1 RIB

To make arrows rib eyelets were cut as shown, and a notch filed for bowstring.

TIC-TACKERS

A SPOOL, A PENCIL AND A PIECE OF STRING — THREE VERY HARMLESS ITEMS, RIGHT?

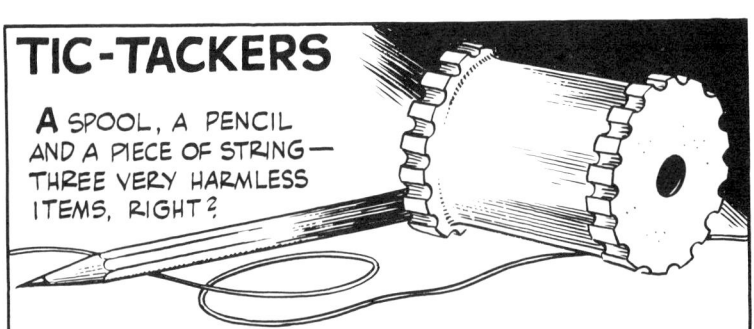

NOTCHES WERE CUT AROUND THE ENDS OF THE SPOOL, THE PENCIL WAS INSERTED THROUGH THE SPOOL, AND THE STRING WAS WRAPPED AROUND THE SPOOL'S CENTER — PRESTO! — YOU HAD A TIC-TACKER. AND WHAT DID YOU DO WITH A TIC-TACKER? YOU PLACED IT AGAINST SOMEONE'S WINDOW AFTER DARK, HELD IT BY THE PENCIL, PULLED THE STRING AND THEN RAN LIKE CRAZY! IT MADE A RACKET THAT SOUNDED LIKE THE HOUSE WAS COMING DOWN!

THE BULL ROARER

THE BULL ROARER WAS A FAMILIAR TOY IN ALL PARTS OF THE COUNTRY. IT WAS SIMPLY A FLAT PIECE OF WOOD WITH A STRING CONNECTED TO A STICK HANDLE. WHEN WHIRLED AROUND THE HEAD IT SANG, EITHER HIGH OR LOW, DEPENDING ON THE SPEED. AS IT WHIRLED AROUND THE HEAD THE FLAT WOOD ALSO ROTATED. THE FLAT PART SHOULD BE ABOUT 2½ BY 6-8 INCHES.

FEATHER EDGES

THE HANDLE COULD BE ANY SMALL STICK; THE STRING SHOULD BE ABOUT 10 OR 12 INCHES LONG. THE FLAT WOOD OUGHT TO BE THIN (ABOUT ¼") AND WORKED BEST IF THE EDGES WERE SANDED TO A FEATHERED FORM.

DANCING DOLLS
THIS WAS THE SORT OF THING THAT MADE YOUR LITTLE SISTER BELIEVE IN MAGIC—

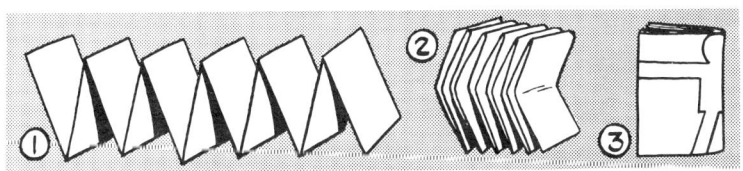

A PIECE OF TISSUE PAPER (¾"×4") WAS FOLDED AS IN ①. THIS WAS SQUEEZED TOGETHER AND FOLDED OVER AT THE CENTER ②, AND LITTLE MEN (OR WOMEN) TRACED ON ③. THESE WERE CUT OUT, GIVING YOU A STRING OF FIGURES... THE FIGURES' FEET (ABOUT ⅛") WERE PASTED ALONG A ⅛" STRIP OF CARDBOARD. FIGURES WERE CUT AS IN ④ AND PLACED IN A CIGAR BOX. THE BOX WAS COVERED WITH CELLOPHANE.

• CUT ON DOTTED LINES

WHEN YOU RUBBED A LITTLE WAD OF SILK OVER THE CELLOPHANE THE FIGURES STOOD UP, AND WHEN YOU TAPPED THE BOX, THEY DANCED LIKE FURIES!

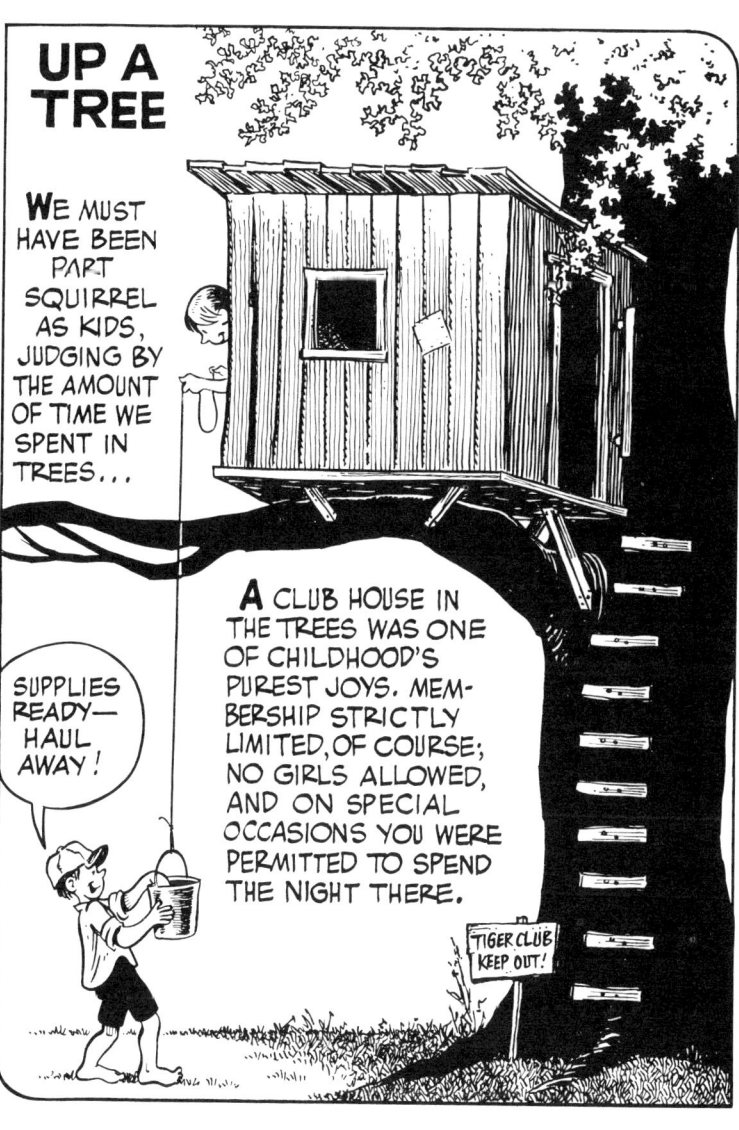

THE CRYSTAL SET

Building a cat's-whisker and crystal radio was one project that required a little help from Pop or an older brother.

The homemade radio receiver was built around a round cardboard oatmeal box. When shellacked and tightly wound with copper wire (which was also shellacked) the box became the coil... The coil was mounted between wooden blocks on a wooden base (the blocks and base shellacked, too.)

Sliders were made from strips of sheet iron with a couple of inches of copper wire soldered to the side that touched the coil... These were mounted on blocks so that one slid along the top of the coil and one along the bottom.

A piece of galena crystal was mounted in a cup with a "cat's whisker" attached above the crystal. Stations were brought in by waving the whisker across the crystal and moving the sliders back and forth along the coil. (We've shown a crystal detector instead of the cat's whisker and crystal. It's easier to get now and works better, if you want to build one today.)

When grounded to a water pipe, hooked up to a rooftop antenna wire, and plugged into earphones, the darn thing actually worked!

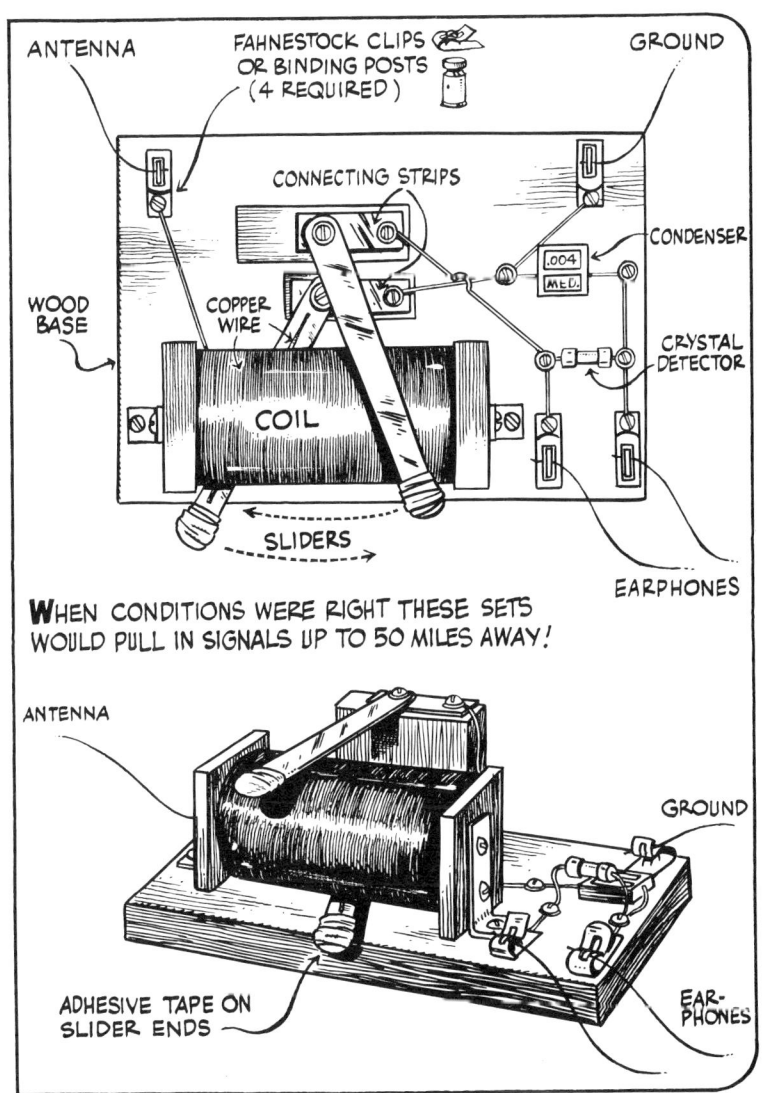

MATCHSTICK DARTS

THIS WAS A GOOD INDOOR GAME AND REQUIRED VERY LITTLE PREPARATION... IN HALF AN HOUR YOU COULD MAKE HALF A DOZEN DARTS AND A TARGET.

SLITS FOR THE NEEDLE AND "FEATHERS" WERE MADE WITH A RAZOR BLADE (ORDINARY KNIFE BLADE WAS TOO THICK AND LIKELY TO SPLIT THE MATCHSTICK).

MODEL AIRPLANE GLUE SECURED THREAD WRAPPING AND WEIGHTED THE DART.

Toss 'em softly... they're very light.

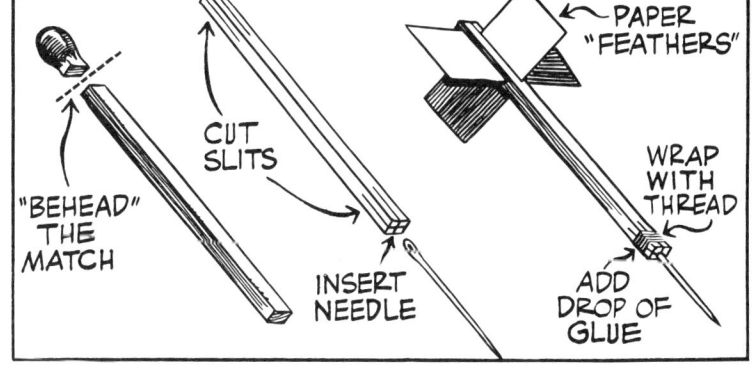

"BEHEAD" THE MATCH — CUT SLITS — INSERT NEEDLE — PAPER "FEATHERS" — WRAP WITH THREAD — ADD DROP OF GLUE

TUBING ALONG TOGETHER

NOBODY EVER WENT TO THE SWIMMING HOLE WITHOUT HIS INNERTUBE (YOU COULD ALWAYS SPOT THE LOCAL RICH KID: HIS DIDN'T HAVE ANY PATCHES!)... INNERTUBES WERE GREAT—THEY HELD YOU UP IF YOU DIDN'T SWIM TOO WELL; YOU COULD DIVE THROUGH THEM (AFTER TAPING DOWN THE VALVE STEM), AND THEY WERE GREAT FOR RACING.

THE WINNER!

WE MADE "TRAINS" BY HOOKING OUR FEET UNDER THE INNERTUBE BEHIND... IF EVERYONE'S PADDLING WAS SYNCHRONIZED (WHICH WAS RARE) PRETTY FAIR SPEED COULD BE ATTAINED.

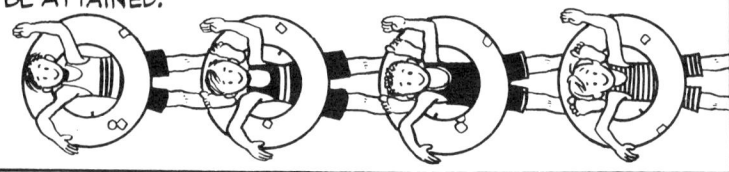

PENNY UGLIES

Among the big items at yesterday's penny candy counter were the "PENNY UGLIES"—— huge red wax lips for girls and buck teeth for boys. After you tired of parading around wearing them, they could be chewed like gum.

"HI, UGLY!"

"LOOK WHO'S TALKING!"

Crossed eyes with the buck teeth made a particularly effective combination!

"JAIL"

"JAIL" WAS A PLAYGROUND OR VACANT LOT GAME THAT REALLY GAVE YOU A WORKOUT. EIGHT GRASS SQUARES WERE LAID OUT AS SHOWN, WITH DIRT PATHS IN BETWEEN. THE DIMENSIONS COULD BE WHATEVER SUITED YOU, AS LONG AS THEY WEREN'T TOO SMALL.

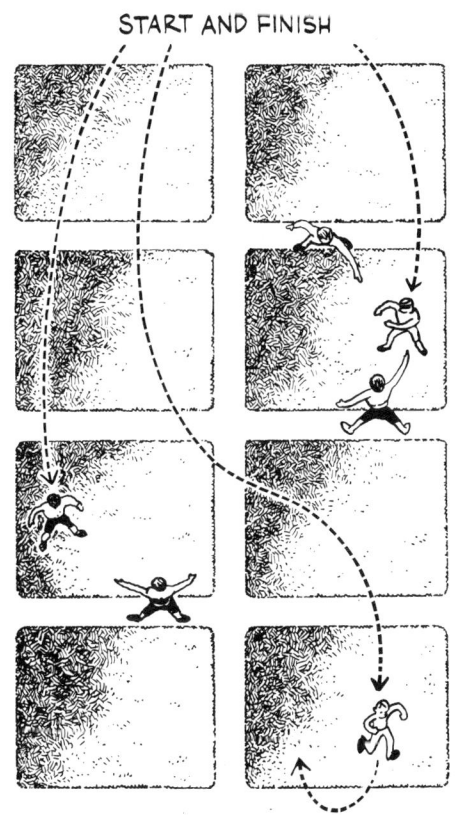

START AND FINISH

"GUARDS" WERE STATIONED IN EACH OF THE PATHS. THEY COULD MOVE IN ANY DIRECTION AS LONG AS THEY STAYED IN THEIR PATHS.

THE OBJECT OF THE GAME WAS TO RUN FROM ONE END TO THE OTHER AND BACK WITHOUT GETTING TAGGED BY A GUARD.

THE GAME GOT TOUGH WHEN TWO GUARDS GOT YOU TRAPPED IN "JAIL" (A SQUARE)... WITH A GUARD REACHING FOR YOU BOTH IN FRONT AND BACK, IT WAS HARD TO DODGE BOTH AND BREAK OUT.

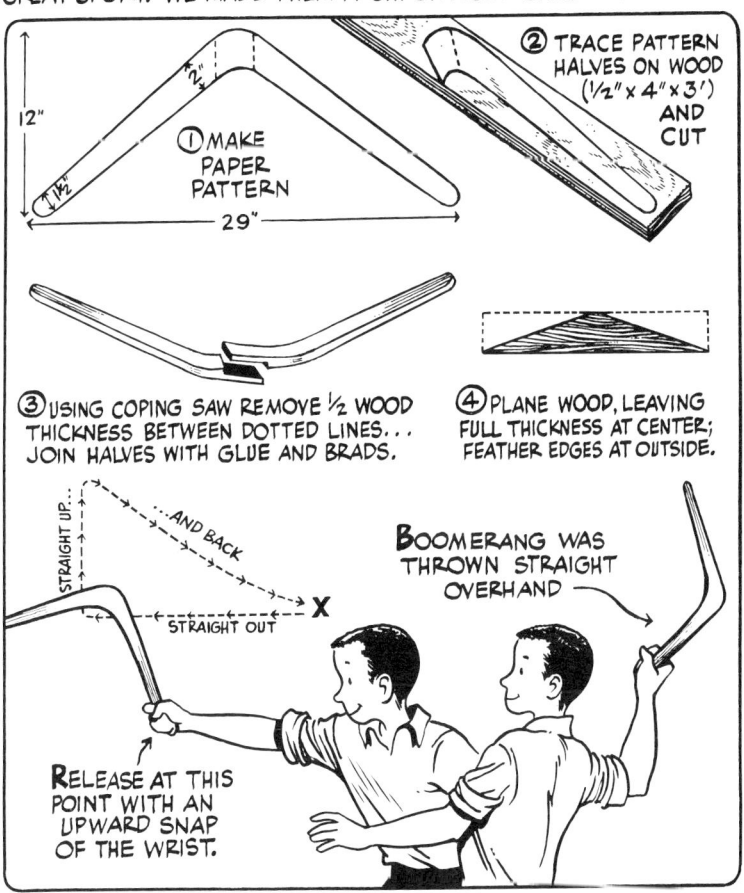

*TOREADOR-A, DON'T SPIT ON THE FLOOR-A,
USE THE CUSPIDOR-A,
THAT'S WHAT IT'S FOR-A!*

WE REALLY BUTCHERED THE CLASSICS WITH OUR SONG PARODIES... ONE OF OUR FAVORITES WAS THIS VERSION OF BIZET'S "TOREADOR SONG" FROM CARMEN... OTHER POPULAR LYRICS WERE:

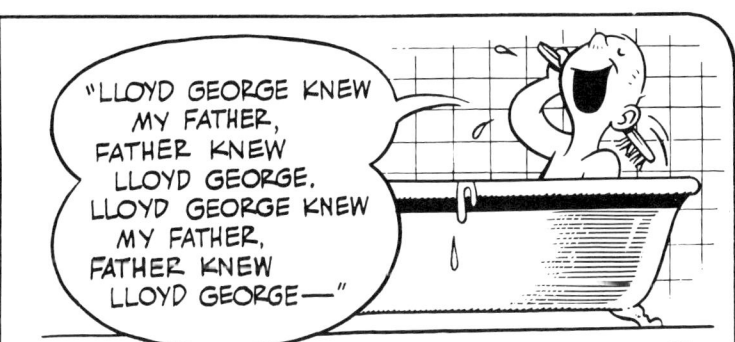

"LLOYD GEORGE KNEW MY FATHER,
FATHER KNEW LLOYD GEORGE.
LLOYD GEORGE KNEW MY FATHER,
FATHER KNEW LLOYD GEORGE—"

(ENDLESSLY REPEATED TO THE TUNE OF "ONWARD CHRISTIAN SOLDIERS".)

"WE THREE KINGS OF ORIENT ARE,
PUFFING ON A LOADED CIGAR—"

"PASSENGERS WILL PLEASE REFRAIN
FROM USING BATHROOMS WHILE THE TRAIN
IS STANDING IN THE STATION,
I LOVE YOU —"

(TO THE TUNE OF "HUMORESQUE". THERE WAS A SECOND VERSE TO THIS ONE — CAN YOU REMEMBER?)

"HERE COMES THE BRIDE,
BIG, FAT AND WIDE,
HERE COMES THE GROOM,
SKINNY AS A BROOM—"

(THIS WAS A MUST WHEN YOU SAW A GUY WALKING WITH A GIRL!)

MAKING A MOTOR

We used to "motorize" our bikes with a clothes pin and a piece of cardboard. Clipped to the fender brace, the cardboard projected into the spokes... the faster you pedaled, the louder and more rapidly the "motor" clicked.

There was only one drawback— you had to stop every so often and tighten the spokes.

THE MUSIC MAKERS

We were all "musicians" of doubtful talent but unbounded enthusiasm!

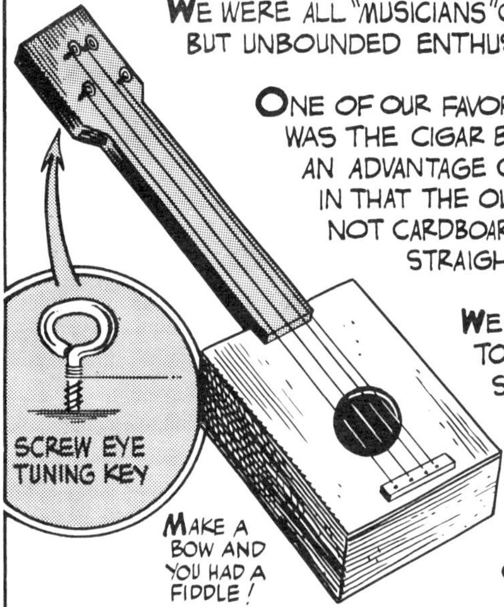

One of our favorite instruments was the cigar box "uke". We had an advantage over today's kids in that the old cigar boxes were not cardboard, but beautiful straight-grained cedar.

SCREW EYE TUNING KEY

Make a bow and you had a fiddle!

We cut a hole in the top, tacked the top shut, added a wood neck, 4 screw eyes for tuning keys, and then strung it. We used real uke strings—you could by them then for a dime apiece.

Other popular "instruments":

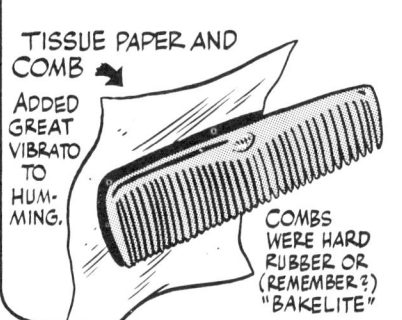

TISSUE PAPER AND COMB

Added great vibrato to humming.

Combs were hard rubber or (remember?) "Bakelite"

The "Juice Harp" or Jew's Harp (steel)

You held it up to your mouth and twanged the spring with your finger.

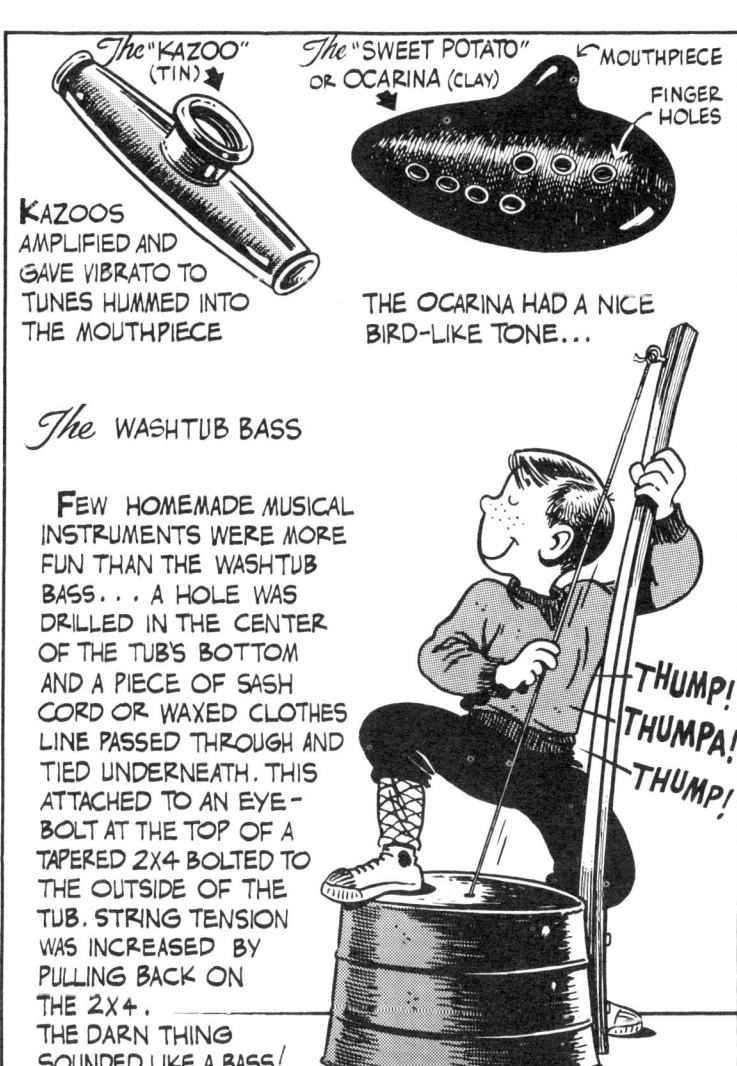

ROUGH RIDERS

APPARENTLY PEOPLE DIDN'T TRADE-IN OLD AUTO TIRES WHEN BUYING NEW ONES 40 YEARS AGO— OLD TIRES COULD BE FOUND ON JUST ABOUT EVERY TRASH HEAP... AND WE SCROUNGED ALL WE COULD FIND FOR VARIOUS PURPOSES...

POSSIBLY THE SILLIEST STUNT WE TRIED WAS RIDING A TIRE DOWN A HILL. USUALLY THIS WAS DONE ON A DARE; WE'D DO ANYTHING RATHER THAN HAVE SOMEONE SAY: "CAN'T YOU TAKE A DARE, 'FRAIDY CAT?"

SO, WE'D CURL UP INSIDE THE TIRE AND TAKE THAT BUMPY, SCARY, TOOTH-RATTLING RIDE DOWN THE HILL!

HOUSE OF CARDS

LARGE RAMBLING STRUCTURES COULD BE BUILT OF PLAYING CARDS, PROVIDED YOU HAD A STEADY HAND. YOU BEGAN BY LEANING THE FIRST CARD AGAINST A TABLE LEG. FROM THEN ON, THE CARDS LEANED ONLY AGAINST THEMSELVES.

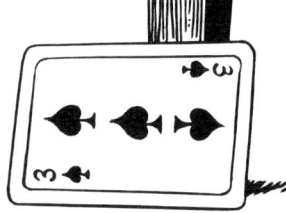

IF YOU WERE ESPECIALLY CAREFUL, MULTI-STORIED BUILDINGS COULD BE MADE. A "GARAGE" WAS ALWAYS ADDED FOR "TOOTSIE-TOY" CARS.

—IF YOU KNOCK MY HOUSE DOWN WITH THAT DUMB CAR, I'M TELLIN'!

VROOM, VROOM!

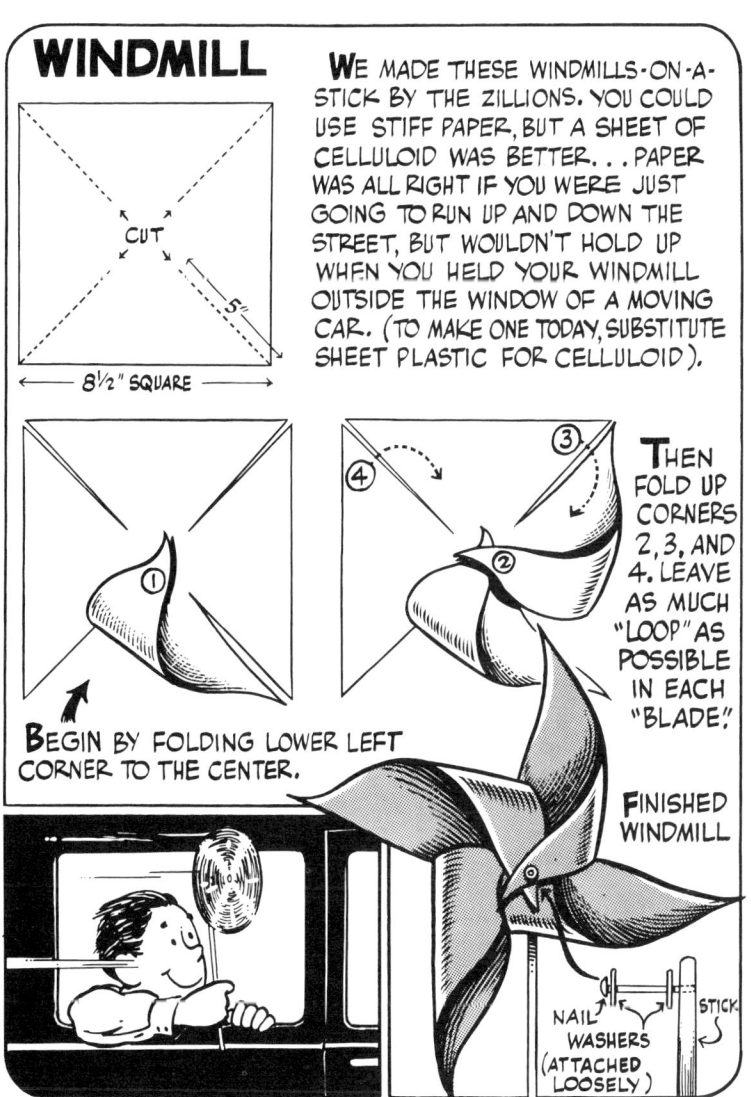

INDIAN CIGARS

CATALPA TREES USED TO BE COMMON LANDSCAPE PLANTS; THEY'RE SELDOM SEEN TODAY. THEY WEREN'T HANDSOME TREES, BUT WE LIKED THEM FOR THEIR LONG, THIN SEED PODS WHICH WE CALLED "INDIAN CIGARS".

WE DIDN'T LIGHT THEM, OF COURSE, BUT THEY WERE IMPORTANT PROPS IN OUR GAMES OF "COPS AND ROBBERS"..."BAD GUYS" ALWAYS SPORTED INDIAN CIGARS AND TALKED OUT OF THE CORNERS OF THEIR MOUTHS.

TINFOIL TYCOONS

CIGARETTES USED TO COME WITH A HEAVY TINFOIL INNER WRAP AND DISCARDED PACKAGES WERE EAGERLY SOUGHT BY KIDS. BACKING PAPER WAS STRIPPED OFF AND THE FOIL WADDED INTO A BALL... CONSIDERABLE STATUS WAS ENJOYED BY THE OWNER OF A LARGE COLLECTION, AND WHEN YOU FINALLY GOT TIRED OF IT, THE FOIL COULD BE SOLD FOR A FEW PENNIES PER POUND TO A JUNK DEALER.

"RED ROVER, RED ROVER...

...SEND 'SKINNY' JONES OVER..." AND SKINNY TOOK OFF AT TOP SPEED TOWARD THE LINE OF KIDS WITH INTERLOCKED ARMS. IF HE BROKE THROUGH THE LINE HE COULD CLAIM ONE OF THEIR MEMBERS FOR HIS TEAM...IF HE FAILED TO BREAK THROUGH, SKINNY HAD TO JOIN THE OPPOSING SIDE...THIS WAS "RED ROVER", AND THE GUYS NEVER CALLED FOR TOUGH "BUTCH" SMITH OR HEFTY "FATSO" BROWN; IT WAS ALWAYS POOR LITTLE "SKINNY" JONES!

FEATHERED FLYERS

This was a dart game—sort of—that we made with chicken feathers, corks and small bits of magnetized metal. The feather was stuck in the large end of the cork and the magnet glued on the other. The target was usually a three pound coffee can...

It wasn't as easy to hit the target as you might think—the flight pattern of these darts was very much like a corkscrew!

SKIP-A-ROPE

THE GIRLS SKIPPED ROPE WITH A VENGEANCE — NOT WITH A SKIMPY LITTLE ONE-GIRL CORD; THEY USED CLOTHESLINE, ABOUT 20 FEET OF IT!... ONE OF THEIR FAVORITE SKIP-SONGS WAS "MY MOTHER SENT ME TO THE GROCERY TO BUY... MILK... EGGS... POTATOES, etc."... A DIFFERENT FOOD FOR EACH SKIP. THE LAST ITEM ON THE GROCERY LIST WAS "HOT PEPPERS"— WHEN "PEPPERS" WAS CALLED, THAT ROPE REALLY FLEW!

N-NOT SO FAST!!

GETTING OUT OF "HOT PEPPERS" REQUIRED DELICATE TIMING; THAT CLOTHESLINE COULD ADMINISTER A NASTY ROPE-BURN!

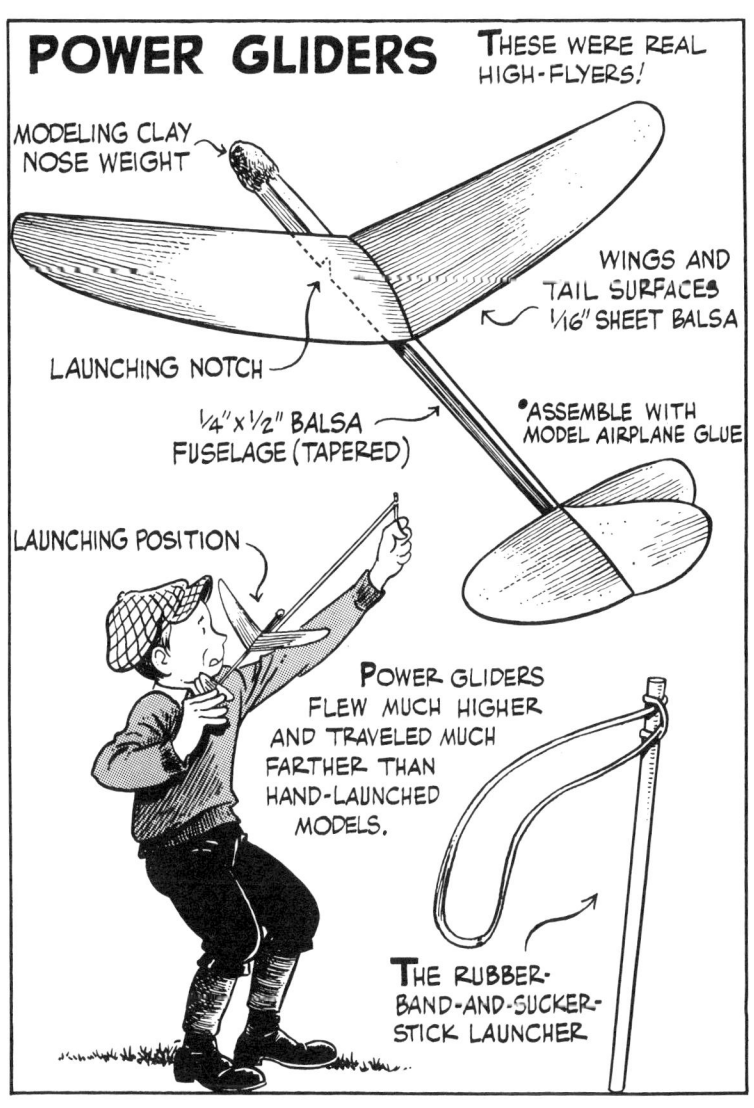

A BUNCH OF YO-YOS

We played with yo-yos: today's kids play with yo-yos. The big difference is that we were in on the ground floor. The yo-yo appeared in America about 1929 (it was native to the Philippines). Merchants used to sponsor Filipino champions who toured playgrounds teaching us "Round-the-World", "Walk the Dog", "Rock the Baby", etc. And each year we entered yo-yo contests.

"ROCK THE BABY"

POSITION FOR "WALK THE DOG", etc.

POSITION FOR "ROUND THE WORLD", "OVER AND UNDER", etc.

You could make a yo-yo, but results were better if you forked over a quarter for a good "spinner".

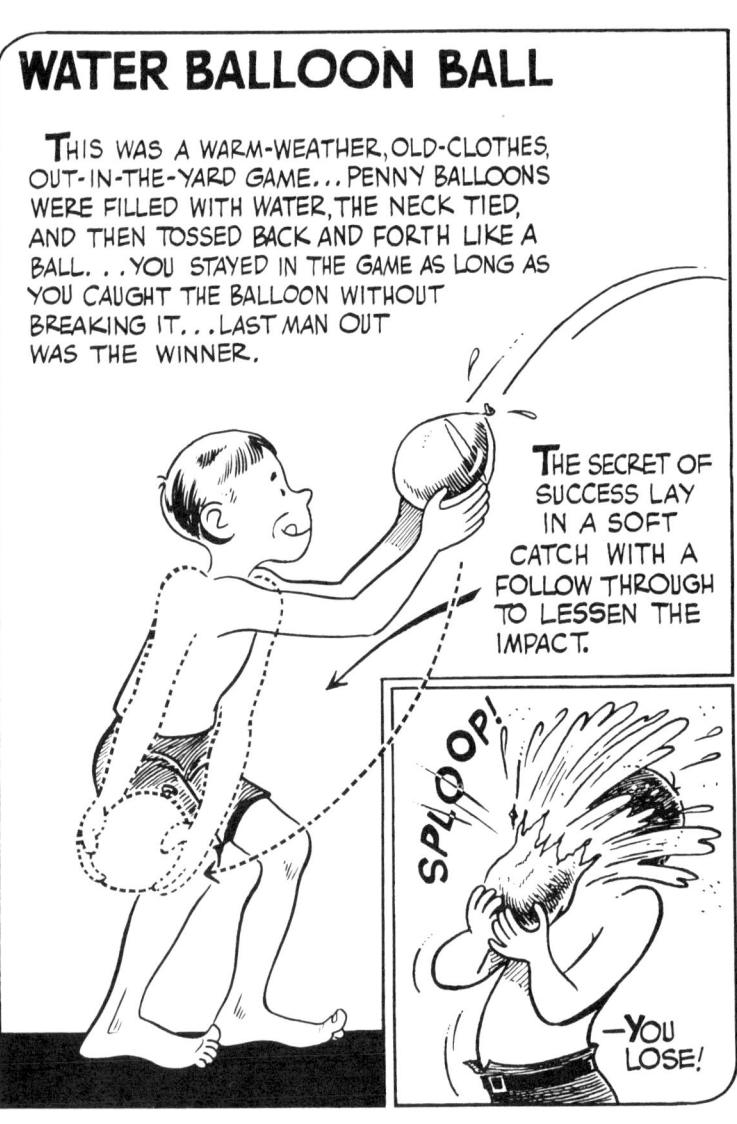

TO BE CONTINUED

HOW WAS IT WHEN YOU WERE A KID ?

We know there were infinite variations of every game kids used to play, and toys were made from every conceivable bit of scrap. If we've left out your favorite pastime from the past, let us know . . maybe you'll be helping to write "HOW TO BE A KID AGAIN, AGAIN". Jot down the way it was with you along with your sketch on this page and send it to :

JIM BAKER---KIDS AGAIN
c/o PERIODS & COMMAS
P.O. Drawer E
Cherry Hill, NJ 08002

Run out of room? O.K. then, use the other side as well.